THE LAUGH JOURNAL

Funny News Stories
from All over the World

Compiled by BUD and LOLO DELANEY
With cartoons by TOM EATON

SCHOLASTIC INC.
New York Toronto London Auckland Sydney

ISBN 0-590-45147-2

12 11 10 9 8 7 6 5 4 3 2 1   1 2 3 4 5 6/9

Printed in the U.S.A.   01

Slim Pickings
For 2 Thieves

CINCINNATI, Ohio (AP) — Albert Lewis was walking to work at the Gibson Greeting Cards Co., when two men in an expensive late-model car pulled onto a driveway ahead of him.

"Give us the paper bag," one man said, pulling a gun and nodding at the bag Lewis carried.

Lewis told the men what was inside.

"Give us the bag," the man insisted. Lewis complied.

The men made their getaway with some work clothes and a ham sandwich.

Reasoning Robber

PORTO ALEGRE, Brazil (AP) — Police said a robbery suspect admitted holding up several taxi drivers, but only because such thievery "pays better and isn't as boring" as his packaging job in a food plant. "I never hurt anybody," he told newsmen as he was being booked. "I detest violence."

She Got Her Man

PRAGUE (AP) — A Czechoslovak housewife set a steel trap for the polecat she thought was stealing eggs from her henhouse. The trap caught the thief, who turned out to be her husband. He confessed he had been stealing the eggs to pay for his drinking.

Mistake 'Weds' Girl To Fiance's Father

PERTH, Australia (AP) — An Australian girl on the way to her wedding reception found she had been married to her father-in-law, at least on paper.

The man sitting beside her in the automobile was her husband all right. Seventy wedding guests here heard Douglas Robertson Shaw, 30 years old, of Fillmore, Calif., pledge to take Miss Helen Haselhurst as his wife.

But when Helen, 24, looked at her wedding certificate, she found the minister had written down the name of the bridegroom's father, Donald Robertson Shaw.

The couple were booked to fly to the United States from Perth. But without a correctly worded certificate, the new Mrs. Shaw could not get a United States visa.

So the witnesses and minister gathered at the honeymoon hotel to sign a fresh certificate.

The bridegroom, who had flown from the United States, had met his bride while working as an electrical engineer, and she as a secretary at the Carnaryon space tracking station.

A Dirty Story

SHEFFIELD, England (UPI) — Janet Marshall left home in a hurry because she was late for her operatic rehearsal. When she opened her case on arrival she found she had brought the weekly wash instead of her costume.

Man Who Gets Boot in Iowa Buys Its Mate in Nebraska

AVOCA, Iowa (AP) — Gary Madden, who wears a 12-EE shoe, finally has a pair of work boots that fit, but it took some doing.

He found a pair the right size in Council Bluffs, Iowa, after having visited a number of stores, but the left one seemed small and closer inspection showed it was a 12-D.

Mr. Madden, 27 years old, then drove to nearby Omaha where, in the parent store of the Council Bluffs store, he found a pair of boots labeled 12-EE. The left one was fine, but the right one did not fit. It turned out to be a 12-D.

He bought the pair of mismatched boots, drove back to Council Bluffs store, and exchanged the right 12-D for the right 12-EE.

Wife, Secretary Have Same Name

WHITSTABLE, England (UPI) — When surveyor Robert Milton goes to work in the morning he kisses Mrs. Sylvia Milton good-bye.

But when he gets to work Mrs. Sylvia Milton is waiting to take a letter.

If he finds he's going to be kept late at the office, he asks Mrs. Milton to get Mrs. Milton on the telephone to tell her so.

His wife and his secretary have the same name.

"When I went for the interview and found that my secretary was a Mrs. Milton, I thought my wife had got a job behind my back," he said.

Not that he would ever have any trouble telling them apart. One is a blonde and the other a brunette.

Dog Didn't Get Chance to Speak

BALTIMORE (AP) — Ronald Lapia pulled his car up to a stoplight in downtown Baltimore. His large English sheepdog was sitting in back.

A man walked up and asked if the dog bit.

Lapia, 30, said the dog did not.

The man pulled out a pistol, forced driver and beast out of the car, and sped off.

"He's a good watchdog in the house, but he's really not very fierce," the victim told police.

'Hit-and-Run' Elephant Let Off in South Africa

PRAETORIA, South Africa (AP) — The National Parks Board plans to take no action against an elephant which trampled an automobile with two tourists inside in Kruger National Park.

The pachyderm was not being held responsible, a board spokesman said, and besides it would be "extremely difficult" to find it among the park's more than 6,000 elephants. The tourists were not injured.

3 Cards With One Thought

EATON RAPIDS, Mich. (AP) — Everyone apparently wanted to wish Mr. and Mrs. John Stair the same thing on their 24th wedding anniversary. The three cards they received — from a nephew in Sunfield, a friend in Leslie, and another friend in Eaton Rapids — had the same design and message.

Hunting Hound Got His Quail; Canned It Too

MEADVILLE, Mo. (AP) — How many hunting dogs will go after a quail and bring back a three-gallon cream can?

Art Heaton of Meadville has one.

Clark Milligan, an assistant at the Fountain Grove Wildlife Area near here, gave this report to the State Department of Conservation:

Milligan and his brother, John, were to meet at Heaton's home.

They arrived to find Heaton's dog wandering around with a three-gallon cream can stuck on its head.

The can wouldn't budge.

They tried a little soap and water. Finally, Clark Milligan drove to Meadville and bought a chisel and hammer.

They got the can off and in it was a dead quail.

It turned out that Heaton had hit the quail with his pickup and it stuck in the grill. He removed the dead bird and tossed it in the can — and the dog went after it.

'Robbery in Reverse' a Puzzle

TULSA, Okla. (UPI) — Jesse Hosey was reluctant to call police the first time it happened. But a month later when an intruder broke into his apartment and, for the second time, instead of stealing anything, left cash, Hosey called authorities.

"I told police it was so screwy I hated to call them," Hosey said Wednesday. The intruder left sixteen dollars November ninth and twelve dollars December tenth and some mysterious writing. "I am concerned about it," Hosey said.

Police were concerned too, but not as much about catching the intruder as what they would do with him afterward.

"By law it can't be classified as a burglary," said investigating officer Ken Moser. "I suppose you could say he was breaking and entering — and then trespassing. That would take care of the intent-to-commit-crime requirement. We have a manhunt on, but I'm just not sure what the charges would be.

"This is definitely a first for me," Moser said. He said Hosey is about 50, works for McDonald-Douglas Aircraft Corp. and "he has plenty."

Wrong Number in Ad Creates 'Run' on Bank

AKRON, Ohio (AP) — Misses Sally Komer, Glendine Irons, and Elsa Mitchell, telephone operators at Akron National Bank, were understandably confused recently when callers said, "I'm calling about your lace panties."

Eventually they discovered that a local department store had placed a newspaper ad for "dainty lace panties in carefree tricot," and would-be purchasers were invited to telephone. But instead of the store's number, the bank's number had been listed by mistake.

She Hits the Gas
Instead of Brake

MILWAUKEE, Wis. (UPI) — Delores Sveum called the turn when, while taking her driver's test, she hit the accelerator instead of the brakes, smashed into a testing station, and injured examiner Alphonse P. Bauer.

"I knew I flunked," she said.

Miss Sveum, 42, was correct but vowed to have another go at it in 10 days.

Wedding Contract Proves Too Formal

HAMLIN, W. Va. (AP) — Suggestions that newlyweds enter into formal marriage contracts, spelling out each party's obligations, are nothing new in southern West Virginia.

A marriage contract on file in the Lincoln County Courthouse since March 11, 1947, declared that the husband, as party of the first part, would be free to come and go as he wished "and not to be spoken against by the party of the second part."

The contract also stipulated that the husband had "full, free, and unmolested control of the home premises, farm, and property, both real and personal."

A clerk at the courthouse, who knew both parties in the contract, said they were divorced a few years later.

Woman Gets Store's Money Along with Her Groceries

AGRA, Kan. (AP) — Mrs. Shirley Buller of Agra drove to Hays, Kansas, a distance of about 65 miles, to get some groceries.

Since she had to drive across a couple of counties to reach the market, she bought a large order. A checkout boy carried out a number of sacks for her.

After Mrs. Butler drove home, she found that the boy had accidentally put into one of the sacks a bag containing cash and checks meant for a Hays bank.

She phoned immediately to the store and an employee rushed to her home to recover the misdirected items.

A Girl in California Spared in Accidents

LAKESIDE, Calif. (UPI) — In 1962, Laurie Clark, of La Mesa, Calif., then only 7 years old, was with her parents when they were killed in an airplane crash near Palm Springs.

Laurie survived.

A few months ago, 17-year-old Laurie was aboard her grandfather's yacht when it went aground and left her and nine others stranded on the Mexican coast 750 miles south of the border.

Laurie survived.

Two months later, Laurie was a passenger in a four-wheel-drive vehicle that overturned on Highway 67 north of Lakeside. The driver, Walter Slunaker, 42, of San Diego — who was captain of the yacht that ran aground — was killed, the California Highway Patrol reported.

Laurie survived.

Wedding for Gypsy Couple Is a Tortuous Ceremony

LUGO, Spain (UPI) — Two young gypsies, a boy from Orense and a girl from Lugo, were married after observing the traditional four-day prenuptial rites of the gypsies.

During these four days the bride was kept locked in her room and the groom chained to the leg of a table.

Meanwhile the guests ate a sheep, four goats, and 30 chickens.

Actor Finds 'Orphanage' Is No Place for Lollipops

SAN FRANCISCO (AP) — Don Frederick, an actor, received a call to report to The Orphanage on Montgomery Street to work on a television series.

En route he stopped at a candy store and bought several dozen lollipops for the kids. He belatedly discovered that The Orphanage was a night club.

Helpmate

ATHENS, Ga. (AP) — Mrs. Jack Curtis lost control of her car yesterday and flattened a 15-by-10-foot sign promoting the Presidential candidacy of George McGovern. Mrs. Curtis is the wife of Jack Curtis, Clarke County Republican chairman. She was not injured.

Snakes Stop a Repairman From Fixing Water Heater

SANTA MONICA, Calif. (UPI) — When Brian Peters, a maintenance man, entered the utility room of an apartment house, all he wanted to do was to fix a water heater.

He lit a match to light the pilot, and in the glow, saw 28 eyes staring back at him — snake eyes.

Mr. Peters called the Santa Monica animal shelter, which sent out a man to round up 14 rattlesnakes, believed to be someone's pets. No one was hurt.

Avid Skiers Are Married on Gondola Lift in Canada

VANCOUVER — Two avid skiers met in the gondola lift at Grouse Mountain. They were single when the lift swung away from the bottom of the mountain, but were man and wife when they got off at the top.

The bridegroom was Ron Williams, coach of the Grouse Mountain Tyee Junior racing team. The bride was Pat Shannon of Dawson Creek, a former national ski team member and a student at the Vancouver School of Art.

Sorry, No Apology

RAWALPINDI (AP) — Management asked 1,500 telephone operators to apologize for their five-day walkout in a contract dispute. The operators went back on strike to protest the request.

Liberation Isn't Everything

LONDON (Canadian Press) — From the personal column of a British daily newspaper: "Harry. Have given up Women's Lib. Please come home. June."

Woman with Snake on Neck Frightens Waitress at Diner

TAMPA, Fla. (UPI) — A waitress at an all-night diner walked over to a booth to take an order from a woman customer, screamed, and then fainted.

Mrs. Marian Jordan, night cashier at the restaurant, told the police the women had a five-foot black snake wrapped around her neck.

Mrs. Jordan said the three persons refused to leave the diner, saying there was no sign stating pets were not allowed.

Disgruntled Bowler Hurls Equipment into the River

OMAHA (AP) — The automobile stopped at midnight on the South Omaha bridge. The driver got out and walked to the railing.

Into the river he pitched a bowling ball . . . and then a bag, then a pair of shoes, then a shirt with lettering across the back.

"He didn't even cuss," a witness one car behind noted.

Extra Wives Are 'Taxing'

KUALA LUMPUR, Malaysia (Reuters) — The Malaysian Parliament rejected a suggestion that Moslems with more than one wife should obtain special income tax relief, after the Deputy Finance Minister said, "If they can afford such a luxury, they should be able to support their additional wife or wives."

Left Waiting

ATHENS (UPI) — Emmanuel Aliesmenakis, 42, waited for two hours at the church in Kolymbari, Crete, Monday before learning that his intended bride, Niki Tzannaki, 30, was in a neighboring village church — getting married to Ionnis Thomadakis, 33, with whom she had eloped.

He 'Bit the Hand' — That Arrested Him

COLOGNE, Germany (UPI) — A 12-year-old boy caught with his loot after he and an older companion broke into a snack bar showed little respect for the forces of law and order, a police spokesman said.

The spokesman said the policeman left the boy alone in the charging room a moment and the youngster stole the officer's sandwiches from a pocket of his uniform and ate them.

Farmer Claims He Nailed Down Record

LONDON (UPI) — Farmer Bernard McCabe, 24, claims a world record for lying on a bed of nails.

He downed a few pints of ale at his local pub, arranged himself gingerly on a nail-studded slab of wood, and stayed there for two hours and 49 minutes — nine minutes more than the reported previous record.

Friendly Car Thief Asks a New Vehicle

SILVER SPRING, Md. (AP) — William Henderson found his stolen car at a service station after a letter mailed to his Washington home told him where it was.

The letter was signed, "Your friendly neighborhood car thief. Get a new car for me."

Henderson, 68, told police he had to pay the service station $25 for work on the car's distributor and battery.

Cradle Is Automated

COCHIN, India (AP) — A new step in automation of baby-sitting is reported by Mitra Das, a 13-year-old schoolboy. Finding it hard to do his homework and rock his baby sister to sleep, he rigged up a microphone device to pick up cradle wails and convert them into electric impulses that activate a motor to rock the cradle.

BABY'S WAILS ARE CARRIED THROUGH EAR TRUMPET (A) TO AWAKEN HIBERNATING BADGER (B) WHO ANGRILY KICKS POLE (C), TIPPING OVER PITCHER (D) AND SPRINKLING WATER ON SQUIRREL (E) WHO THINKS IT'S RAINING AND TRIES TO RUN FOR COVER. TREADMILL WORKS BELLOWS (F) TO PRODUCE SIGHING SOUND—PEACOCK (G) BELIEVES HE IS BEING ADMIRED AND SPREADS HIS TAIL—FIREFLIES IN GLOBE (H) MISTAKE TAIL FOR EYES OF ANIMALS IN DARKNESS AND ALL LIGHT UP, POWERING MOTOR (I) WHICH MOVES ARM (J) AND ROCKS CRADLE.

Two Chimpanzees Live in Attorney's Home

SEMINOLE, Fla. (AP) — Marc, six years old, digs heavy rock, watches television, and, when asked, puts clothes in the dryer and turns it on.

Marc is a chimpanzee who lives at the Alan Williams' home with another chimp named Sina, who is 3½ years old. Marc lives in his own room modishly decorated with tires and ropes.

"I've conditioned them to home living," said Mr. Williams, a 39-year-old attorney.

He feels raising chimps in a human home isn't cruel.

"If I didn't have them here, they'd be in a zoo or laboratory," he asserted. "Marc, from all I've read, is probably the oldest chimp raised in a home environment."

Saves Tree from Ax
By Pledge to Perch

NEWARK, England (AP) — Note for those who think conservationists should go climb a tree: Andrew Boggie did so Monday and spared a 200-year-old elm from the ax.

The 44-year-old mailman perched 30 feet up in the venerable elm and declared he would stay there during his entire month of vacation to keep the Newark council from felling the tree to make room for a soccer field.

The council held a special meeting and decided to put the soccer field elsewhere.

Baby Named After Bus

MANILA (Reuters) — A young Filipino housewife gave birth to a baby boy on a bus near Manila, and named him after the bus. Mrs. Gloria Munoz, 28 years old, said it was a "Victory Liner" bus so she called him Victor.

It Was Just
A Blinkin' Crime

SOUTHEND-ON-SEA, England (UPI) — Police were baffled at why the burglar alarm at a tailor shop rang.

They searched the shop without finding anything, then as they were leaving one noticed that one of the mannequins in the display window blinked.

John McDaid, the unsuccessful burglar, pleaded guilty to burglary and was fined $23.50 and given a six-month suspended sentence.

4-Year-Old's View of Sister

SPARTANBURG, S.C. (AP) — Four-year-old Jan Porter was asked if she knew what a sister was. Jan, who has an older sister, Caroline, 5, paused for a moment to consider. "A sister," she finally replied, "is a little girl who grows up to be your sister — but not your friend."

Stubborn Virginian 'Breaks Into' Jail

ROANOKE, Va. (AP) — A Roanoke man found to his temporary dismay that it can be mighty hard to get into the city jail.

He walked up to a policeman and asked to be put in jail for Christmas.

The policeman suggested that the man contact appropriate agencies for help.

The man insisted that he wanted to go to jail. The policeman refused.

The man pulled a bottle out of his pocket and smashed a store window.

The store manager came out of the store, was told what had happened, and said he did not want to press charges because it was too close to Christmas.

Finally, 29-year-old Walter P. Rose was taken to jail on a charge of disorderly conduct.

Man, 107, Sentenced to Six Years in Jail

VITORIA, Brazil (AP) — Pedro Pereira da Silva, 107, has been sentenced here to six years in prison.

Da Silva was accused of having a son-in-law killed by hired gunmen.

Brazil has lenient legal punishment for persons older than 70 but in the da Silva case the prosecution asked for a severe sentence because he was found in perfect physical and psychological condition at the age of 104, when he was indicted.

Da Silva's lawyer, however, said he would appeal for an acquittal or lighter sentence because of his client's advanced age.

Parachutist Leaps Into Matrimony

SINGAPORE (UPI) — Singapore army commando Maj. Chan Seck Sung literally dropped in at his own wedding.

Chan, 27, a member of the Parachutist Association of Singapore, was scheduled to make a 4,000-foot jump from an aircraft. It was also the day for his marriage to Miss Lim Hui Ai, also 27.

So he donned a jumpsuit over his ceremonial army uniform and jumped, landing a few feet from the training center where Miss Lim and guests were waiting. They were married immediately and a reception was held at a nearby officers' mess.

Duck Is Renamed

CHICAGO (AP) — Ernest, mascot of the Salt Creek Golf Club and pet of the family of Earl Schmidt, club manager, has been renamed Ernestine. The white duck's secret came out when it deposited nine eggs around the grounds of the golf course.

Driver Denied Parking Spot Takes It Out on 'Road Hog'

SEATTLE (UPI) — When Miss Judy A. Frost returned to a parking lot to get her automobile after work, she found the windshield smashed and a note telling her why.

The note berated her for allowing her car to straddle a dividing line.

The angry motorist, in addition to smashing the woman's windshield with a block of concrete, also removed the coil and distributor cap from her engine.

Action Is Repeated by Drunken Driver

LOS ANGELES (AP) — Fred Lakins, a 31-year-old liquor salesman from Monterey, didn't make it past the courthouse steps when he drove to Van Nuys to answer a charge of drunken driving, authorities said.

William Rossiter, a courthouse guard, said Mr. Lakins drove his car across 100 feet of courthouse lawn, forcing two women to jump to safety, and then bumped up the front steps.

"I came to pay a drunk-driving ticket," Mr. Rossiter said, Mr. Lakins told him. "I might just as well prove the point."

Mr. Lakins, arrested in San Fernando a month before on a charge of drunken driving, was booked again for investigation of motoring under the influence of alcohol, authorities said.

Youth Hijacking
A Bus Comes
To Sudden Stop

TORONTO (Canadian Press) — There have been hijacks and skyjacks and recently Toronto experienced its first busjack.

The driver of a Toronto Transit Commission bus left the vehicle for a few minutes to get a coffee, prompting a youthful passenger to jump into the driver's seat and drive off.

When the driver realized what was happening, he jumped back aboard and pulled a power switch. The bus crashed into an excavation for a subway station, causing about $1,000 damage but no one was injured.

Chimp Blacks
Out Circus

LONDON (AP) — Minutes before a circus show was due to be staged at a concert hall, all the lights in the auditorium went out. Frantic electricians located the fault. A chimpanzee had thrown the master switch.

Robbers Serve Customers

REDDING, Calif. (UPI) — Two unsuspecting women customers walked into a shoe store as two armed men were robbing it. One of the men calmly waited on the women, then both escaped with $145 and two pairs of shoes.

Couple Finds a Cat Sealed Into Roof of Mobile Home

LOS ANGELES (AP) — Mr. and Mrs. Gerald Hendrick spent several sleepless nights in their new mobile home because of mysterious thumping noises on the roof.

They checked the roof, but there was nothing on it. After further investigation, they found that a full-grown cat had been sealed into the roof by mistake, apparently when the vehicle was at the factory about two weeks before.

When it was taken out, the cat proved to be in good condition, except that it had a ravenous appetite and ferocious thirst.

Bird Spies for Indian Army

AHMADABAD, India (AP) — A member of the State Assembly said soldiers had told him that a tiny bird known as the Babbler got excited and "babbled" any time there was a troop movement on the other side of the border.

Failure on Dowry Costs Turk a Wife

ISTANBUL, Turkey (AP) — Arguing that goods not paid for can be taken back, a man in Nusaybin, south-eastern Turkey, has reclaimed his daughter because her husband had defaulted in his dowry payments.

Aziz Koc, 36 years old, a hospital janitor, paid $350 down and promised to pay $70 a year for five years when he married Saha Gelir three years ago.

When he missed the third payment, Saha's father raided his house and took back his daughter and her three-year-old son, apparently as interest.

"When it came to the money, he tried to get off light," the father said. "But I won't let him get away with it."

Mr. Koc was trying to get a loan from his employers to buy back his wife.

Thief Tells Policeman Bank Alarm Is 'False'

NITEROI, BRAZIL (UPI) — The police received an alarm signal indicating a robbery was underway at the Mercantile and Industrial Bank.

When a policeman telephoned the bank to check, one of five bandits inside answered and calmly said it was a false alarm.

The five bandits then continued their robbery and got away with $3,700.

Cat Likes to Play Frisbee

REDLAND, Ore. (AP) — Rusty, a seven-month-old tomcat, is a Frisbee enthusiast. The Jack Kragers, its owners, said the cat started to catch the plastic disc some time ago, and since then has rarely refused to play. The cat at one time played with the family for more than two hours, they said.

Request for Medicare Form Brings Woman Two Cartons

POMPANO BEACH, Fla. (AP) — A Pompano Beach woman who believed in the adage "ask and you shall receive" got a lot more than she requested when she wrote the Social Security office for an extra copy of a medicare form.

A week later, a truck pulled up to her door and deposited two cartons of the requested forms.

With 1,999 extras, she made the rounds of the neighbors giving away hundreds. But still, there were leftovers.

She called the Social Security office and it sent out another truck to pick up the spare copies.

"We thought she was an office," a Social Security spokesman explained.

Their Divorce Is on the Rocks

ROMFORD, England (UPI) — Maureen and Gordon Felton got a divorce last week. Today they said they were planning to marry again.

"We both realize that after 12 years of marriage we can't live without each other," Gordon said.

Minor Injuries, Major Worry

SANDY, Utah (AP) — Stanford McDonald, 5, rode his bicycle in front of a car and suffered minor injuries.

He looked up tearfully from a stretcher taking him to a hospital and asked his parents:

"Do you think they'll give me a ticket?"

Police assured him they wouldn't.

An Infant Attends Classes At College

YAKIMA, Wash (AP) — Karlyn Hurlburt has logged more classroom time than half the freshman class at Yakima Valley College.

She is less than a year old and spends most of her academic time in an apple carton.

Carl and Sue Hurlburt, Karlyn's parents, both students at the college, decided being parents didn't have to interrupt their education. Mr. Hurlburt is majoring in agribusiness, his wife in pre-education.

Karlyn and her apple box have been a regular fixture in the college's classrooms since September, when she was three weeks old.

"It was either bring her with us every day or have one of us stay at home with her and miss a year of college," said Mrs. Hurlburt.

If Mr. Hurlburt has a free period, he looks after Karlyn in a hallway while his wife attends class and vice versa.

If both of the 20-year-old parents have simultaneous classes, Karlyn accompanies one of them.

"The baby has been no trouble or disruption at all," said John Griffith, head of the college agriculture department. "She seems to know she is supposed to sit quietly while the teacher delivers the lecture."

Bad Luck 'Dogs' Californian On His Way Home With Cake

SAN FRANCISCO (UPI) — One housewife may not have received a valentine this year, although her husband bought her a special cake for the day.

En route home with the gift, the unidentified man ran afoul of the traffic laws and was stopped by a motorcycle officer, Homer H. Hudelson.

After arguing awhile with Mr. Hudelson, the man accepted a citation and went back to his car to find that a dog had climbed into the back seat and eaten the cake.

Parachutist Gets 'Hung Up' as Sock Catches on Plane

SYDNEY, Australia (AP) — Keith Lancaster, a parachutist, jumped from a small plane over Sydney, fell three feet, and then one of his socks caught on the step beside the plane's wheel.

He hung there upside down for 10 minutes before another parachutist in the plane managed to cut him free with a jagged piece of metal he had torn from an aircraft seat.

The 36-year-old Mr. Lancaster landed safely. He has made more than 100 jumps.

A Ring Lost 14 Years Ago Is 'Found' by Cow in France

LORIENT, France (UPI) — Xavier Magnan recently recovered a gold ring he had lost in a field 14 years ago thanks to a limping cow owned by a neighbor, Pierre Nicolas.

When Mr. Nicolas decided to find the cause for his cow's limp, he found the ring, bearing his neighbor's name, embedded in the animal's hind hoof.

Sorry Surname

MELUN, France (AP) — A judge who refused to saddle a 3-year-old boy with what he considered a ridiculous surname earned the indignation of the child's adopted parents plus an appeal to a higher court. Their name is Trognon, a word meaning stump, rag-end, core, or the little piece left over that you throw away.

Burglar Goes Back to Prison Luxuries

WELLINGTON, New Zealand (AP) — New Zealand prisons are nothing more than rest homes, according to a convicted burglar, Peter Apotoru Maru.

Appearing in Wellington Magistrate's Court on seven counts of burglary, the 32-year-old Mr. Maru told the bench:

"These places you call prisons are no longer prisons. To me, they are only rest homes. People who are sent there have better meals than in most of your hotels."

Mr. Maru said there were other luxuries that would not make a person like himself change his ways.

Stipendiary Magistrate Benjamin Scully sent Mr. Maru back to jail for 12 months for his latest offenses.

A Justice Department official said:

"We are pleased to have the commendation on our prisons. Usually, inmates are quick to complain about the standard of meals provided."

A Black Bird Flies
Out of Toilet Bowl

MILWAUKEE (AP) —
When Mrs. James Spiel-
vogel was cleaning her bath-
room recently, a black bird,
possibly a starling, emerged
from the toilet bowl, hopped
up on the seat, shook off the
water, then fluttered to the
floor.

"I screamed bloody mur-
der," Mrs. Spielvogel said.
"And if it hadn't been just
an ordinary black bird, I'd
probably still be standing
there screaming."

Robert Flint, superin-
tendent of plumbing inspection for the city said his
files were full of cases of
rats, snakes, and even a
squirrel making the trip
down sewer vent-pipes from
the tops of houses and eventually out through toilet
bowls.

Oregon Hen Picks Own Spot For 'Planting' of Her Eggs

CARVER, Ore. (AP) — A pet hen at the Sara Wickham home is very particular about where she lays her eggs.

She refuses to lay them in the cardboard box provided outdoors. When the "urge" comes, she steps to the back door, pecks on the door until she is admitted, marches across a room to a planter in which a rhododendron is growing, and lays an egg.

She then hops out of the planter, struts across the floor to the back door, and waits for someone to let her outdoors again.

Bear Nabbed
As Jaywalker

MONTPELIER, Vt. (AP) — Police say an unidentified caller told them there was a jaywalker at Colonial Drive and Northfield Street in the center of town.

They went to the scene Saturday night and found the jaywalker, but they didn't arrest him. They chased him away.

The culprit was a small black bear.

Man Is Robbed of $80 And Given $790 Watch

ST. LOUIS (UPI) — Three men robbed Claude West of $80 on a recent Saturday, then gave him a $790 watch.

Mr. West, a district supervisor for the American Telephone & Telegraph Company, told the police he was getting into his car when the men called him.

He walked over to their car and the driver pointed to a revolver on the seat. Mr. West gave them his money and the driver handed him a case with an Omega watch in it, saying it was "clean." The police said the watch was worth $790.

What's In a Name?

SYDNEY, Australia (AP) — A parked station wagon with a sign on it reading "Mafia Staff Car — Hands Off" has remained unmolested.

Pigeon Back After
Four Years

PORTSMOUTH, England (UPI) — A racing pigeon flew home to its loft here four years after its owner sent it to race back from Durham, 300 miles away.

A Clerk at City Hall
Helps Keep Wedding
On Schedule

BROCKTON, Mass. (AP) — City Clerk John Lyons played assistant to Cupid recently when he went to the City Hall on a Saturday, opened the vault, and got a marriage license for Ernest Cugno and Diane Washek.

In the haste of wedding preparations, Mr. Cugno, a serviceman just back from Viet Nam, and his bride forgot to pick up the license for the Sunday wedding before the City Hall closed for the weekend.

Woman in a Cardboard Box Sits In at Colorado Senate

DENVER (AP) — A large cardboard box staged a sit-in at the Colorado State Senate.

An unidentified woman, covered from head to hip by a large cardboard box, walked into the Senate. The box carried the legend "Senators — you were elected by the people — not the billboard industry." It was an apparent protest against the lack of more restrictive billboard legislation.

The woman, who said she was "Mrs. Taxpayer," declared:

"A billboard in a green field is just like a moth hole in a beautiful garment."

Baby Refuses to 'Play Bawl' With British Drama Group

WATFORD, England (Canadian Press) — When an amateur actress, Mrs. Lynda Savory, had a baby, the local dramatics group was delighted — the child would provide the recorded sound effects for their latest play.

But since rehearsals began, six-month-old baby Alan hasn't shed a tear for the tape recorder, which is switched on day and night.

"My husband and I haven't had a quieter time for months," Mrs. Savory said. "It looks as if Alan won't play bawl."

House a British Fireman Seeks To Save Is His Own

STOWMARKET, England (UPI) — When the alarm came in to the Stowmarket Fire Department, Phil Dade, a fireman, did not have to think twice how best to get to the blaze — it was his own house.

But it was only a minor fire, and his wife extinguished it before he and the other firemen arrived.

Teen-aged Girl Is Elected Church Elder In Knoxville

KNOXVILLE, Tenn. (AP) — The congregation of Knoxville's Westminster Presbyterian Church named Miss Susan Crenshaw, a premedical student, to the Board of Elders, highest governmental body in the local church.

A spokesman for the denomination said that several young males had been elected elders in recent years but that Miss Crenshaw may be the first teen-aged female to fill that position.

A Missouri Woman Learns 'Key' Facts About Handcuffs

ST. LOUIS (AP) — Miss Karen Hickey had often wondered how it felt to be handcuffed. She found out the hard way.

The 22-year-old secretary tried on old handcuffs found and brought to the office by her boss, and remained handcuffed for two hours until firemen working with electric cutters freed her.

"Next time, I'll ask first if there are any keys," Miss Hickey said.

Lost Cat Is Found at Paper That Carries Ad About It

NAPANEE, Ontario (Canadian Press) — Miss Naomi McDonald advertised in area newspapers when her Siamese cat, Ching, disappeared.

Three months later Miss McDonald received a call from the editor of the *Qunite Scanner,* one of the papers in which she had put the ad, and learned that Ching had just been found alive and well — in the basement of the newspaper's printing shop.

An Inept Car Thief Told to Try New Field By Judge

PITTSBURGH (UPI) — Judge Richard McCormick had some words of advice for a man he convicted recently on burglary charges.

"You make a pretty rotten burglar," Judge McCormick told 24-year-old Guy E. Bertini of Pittsburgh. "You have been caught twice in cars. That should convince you that besides being illegal, burglary isn't your field."

In each case, the police said, Mr. Bertini was spotted inside the cars he was charged with burglarizing. He fled from one, but left a signed application for a mortgage loan on the floor of the car.

German Boy 'Digs' Cash

SILTORF, Germany (UPI) — Digging in a field near this north German village, Peter Poertzen, 8, found nearly one million Russian rubles in a milk can stuffed to the brim with five-ruble notes, police said.

A paymaster of the Nazi Wehrmacht was believed to have buried the treasure in the closing days of World War II.

What Do You Say to Man Carrying a 'Naked Lady'?

PHOENIX, Ariz. (AP) — How do you carry a naked lady around a department store?

"Very carefully," says Robert Severance, whose job it is to assemble, dress, and transport mannequins at a local department store.

"You'd be amazed at the remarks people come up with when they see a man carrying a mannequin through the store — 'How's your girl friend?' 'That's no way to treat a lady,' or they just stare, point, and laugh," he said.

Commencements Just His Thing

PUYALLUP, Wash. (AP) — Don Anderson, 19, took part in his second graduation ceremony at Rogers High School, handing out diplomas this week as a member of the school board.

Dressed in the same blue sport coat he bought for his own commencement a year ago, Anderson distributed sheepskins to friends and former classmates, and afterwards admitted it felt "a little strange."

Anderson was a member of the first graduating class at the new high school and five months later was elected to the school board. He is a student at the University of Oregon 260 miles to the south in Eugene but has been able to attend most school board meetings this year.

Woman Has Trouble 'Banking' on Lamps

MEDFORD, Mass. (UPI) — A Massachusetts woman may not be so sure now that lampshades are safer than banks.

The woman, who did not want to be identified, said that she had been stitching her savings into the linings of lampshades since the 1930s.

"I'm not crazy or anything, it just seems to me that lampshades are safer than banks," she said.

Recently, she said, she forgot which lampshades had the money and threw out two of them containing a total of $2,500.

Sanitation workers had picked up the rubbish and were leaving the woman's street when she ran up to them and explained the situation.

The workers went to the dump, emptied the contents of their truck, and spent half an hour sifting through the junk. They found the lamp-shades and the money.

"I'm thankful there are good, clean, honest men working for the city of Medford," the woman said.

"I guess that's all the thanks we needed," said Victor Ferri, sanitation yard foreman.

Marriage Gets 'Cold Start' on The Ice of Lake St. Clair

HARRISON TOWNSHIP, Mich. (AP) — Miss Pamela Benning and Jack Carlson were married recently on the ice of Lake St. Clair, a body of water separating Canada from the United States.

"Pamela is originally from Toronto," Mr. Carlson explained, "and I was born in Detroit. So we decided to have the wedding in between. In this way, we hope to have no national differences affect our relationship."

The bride, bridegroom, and attendants all wore snowmobile suits for the occasion.

30 Cents in Taxes Costs 40 Cents for Exchanges

PHILLIPSBURG, Kan. (AP) — An elderly Phillips County woman who owed 30 cents in intangible property tax has proved that collections can sometimes be expensive.

The lady and the county spent a total of 40 cents in postage in swapping tax statements, payments, and receipts.

The county mailed the lady a bill for 30 cents and she paid the first half of it, using an eight-cent stamp as the county had done in sending her bill. The county mailed her a receipt. She then decided to pay the remaining 15 cents for the other half of her tax and was mailed a "paid in full receipt."

Fish Bites Dog, Man Saves Dog

SUDBURY, England (UPI) — Barney, a 98-pound German shepherd, was having his daily paddle in a lake Monday when a huge pike clamped its jaw on his leg and almost pulled him under.

Barney's master, Tony Wright, said he hauled the three-year-old dog to safety with the 15-pound pike still clamped on Barney's leg. The pike then let go and flopped back into the water.

"A smaller dog would have drowned," Wright said.

Timely Fire Helps Driver Prove Point

SAN FRANCISCO (AP) — George Merritt was stopped by a highway patrolman because his tow truck didn't have the required fire extinguisher.

Mr. Merritt explained that his fire extinguisher had been stolen, but that meanwhile he was prepared for any fire with an old army blanket.

"Very funny," said the officer, taking out his book.

Just then an auto burst into flames across the road. A fire extinguisher was pulled out but didn't work.

Mr. Merritt dashed over with his blanket and smothered the fire.

"You win," said the patrolman, shaking his head. "No tag."

Youthful Angler Hooks Himself

When 10-year-old Mike Rooney set out Thursday to catch the "big one" at the Six Mile Waterworks, little did he think it would be himself.

The youngster, who lives at 176 Sycamore St., was at the popular fishing spot when he waved his pole and the hook was imbedded in the back of his head.

Albany police took him to St. Peter's Hospital where the hook was removed leaving no scar — only a fisherman's damaged ego.

A 'Tarzan and Jane' Hang Around In Tree

PORT ARTHUR, Tex. (Reuters) — Dave Smith, a patrolman, spotted a couple sitting in a tree.

"Who are you and what are you doing?" he asked them.

"I'm Tarzan," said the young man although he was fully dressed.

"And I am Jane," said the woman.

"Oh, yeah, then where's Cheetah?" asked the officer.

The couple then produced their pet chimpanzee, who had been romping on a higher limb. Unamused, the officer ordered them to climb down and go home, which they did, leading their pet on a leash.

Coins Get Stuck in Machine, So Does a 9-Year-Old Boy

SALT LAKE CITY (AP) — Nine-year-old Bob Rowlands did not like the idea of losing 15 cents in a soft drink machine.

So he went after it — up to his elbow.

It took maintenance men, vending machine operators, and firemen four hours to free him.

'Ghost' Cuts Out Overtime

CHERTSEY, England (AP) — Workers at a printing factory in Surrey have banned overtime until the management can banish Henry, a ghost, from the shop floor. The men refuse to stay in the building after dark, when, they claim, Henry opens and closes locked doors.

No Bill, He Had a Plain Old Nose

LOUISVILLE, Ky. (AP) — While John Bockey was writing checks to pay a batch of bills, the doorbell rang and it was answered by his daughter, Mary.

She announced that a man wanted to see him.

"What's he got, a bill?" sighed Bockey.

"No," replied his daughter, "he's just got a plain old nose."

A Talking Bird, And Rude Too

LEVITTOWN, Pa. (AP) — Middletown Township police say they are trying to apprehend a talking blackbird.

Police said the bird has been buzzing and diving at children near an elementary school in the township for several days.

Officers claim the bird can say "Hello" and "Bug off."

Tuesday, the bird was reported spotted perched atop the roof of the school cawing "Bug off" to a township animal control officer who was trying to capture it.

Robber's Apology Lands Him in Jail

CHICAGO — Henry Cohen may never say he's sorry to anyone ever again — and love doesn't have anything to do with it.

The 17-year-old Henry was arrested after he mailed back the wallet he stole from a 23-year-old secretary — along with a polite note apologizing for attacking her and asking her to call him at his home, police said.

He even included his telephone number.

Miss Sheila Sink called police instead.

Burglars Are Successful Despite Efforts of a Parrot

HAMMOND, Ind. (AP) — Polly put up a good fight, but burglars still got more than $1,000 in belongings and cash from the Patrick O'Meara residence here.

When the police arrived they found a trail of feathers leading to the door.

Mrs. O'Meara said Polly, a 5-year-old parrot, was very talkative and friendly.

"With all the feathers around he must have put up a good squabble," she said.

"He knew all our friends' names and could sing an Irish song or two. I hope he isn't hurt."

Talk About the Final Word, a Tombstone 'Tells It All'

SAN ANTONIO, Tex. (AP) — Sister Margaret Rose Palmer of Incarnate Word College here has found what must be the ultimate in having the last say-so.

Visiting historical sites while at Harvard last summer, she spotted a tombstone in an old cemetery at Plymouth, Mass., with this inscription:

"I told you I was sick, Elizabeth!"

Some Food for Thought

SPARTANBURG, S. C. (AP) — A sign on a local home reads: "Salesmen Welcome — Dog Food Is Expensive."

Test Drive 'Sold' Car

BRADFORD, England (UPI) — A salesman at a Bradford automobile showroom took a well-spoken young man in a pin-striped suit for a demonstration drive recently in an expensive BMW coupe after the man said he might buy the car.

When they stopped at a traffic light, the would-be customer asked if he could drive the car. When the salesman got out to change places, the young man slid behind the wheel and sped off. Police said the car and driver have not been seen since.

Collie Prefers Life at Pound

PLYMOUTH, England (UPI) — Randy the collie is perfectly happy living in the dog pound.

Manager Ken Taylor has sold Randy 11 times, each time for $7.80, and 11 times Randy has come back.

Sex Fights Stress

TOKYO (AP) — Researchers for the Japan National Railway have concluded that sex can fight stress at rush hour. They recommended that male passengers get as close as possible to attractive passengers in crowded commuter trains. No advice was offered to women.

Conscience of Ex-Employee Nets Wyoming Company One Dollar

SHERIDAN, Wyo. (AP) — A man walked into the Holly Sugar Company's agricultural research station here and handed the secretary a one-dollar bill.

He explained that many years ago, while employed as a sugar loader, he used to take small quantities of sugar home in his lunch box. He wanted to pay for the sugar.

The plant at Sheridan has not produced any sugar since 1948.

Couple Marries
On Horses

SAUGUS, Calif. (UPI) — Jack Threet and Dorothy Esser rode off into the sunset together after they had been married while sitting astride their horses at a local stable. The 51-year-old Mr. Threet and Miss Esser, 45, who fell in love while riding horses, leaned over in their saddles and kissed one another, as they were pronounced married.

British Woman Puts
Glitter into Smile
with Diamonds

BIRMINGHAM, England (UPI) — Miss Katherine Ray, 18 years old, has a smile that glitters — literally.

Miss Ray walked into a dentist's office, sat down, and asked for eight diamonds to be fitted to her gold tooth caps.

The dentist and a jeweler got together and produced what the jeweler described as "a beautiful mouthful which will last a lifetime."

Big-Time Spender Picks Wrong Place

BOWLING GREEN, Ky. (UPI) — James Whitney picked the wrong place to spread his money around. He entered a courtroom in Warren Circuit Court recently and began handing out dollar bills.

The demonstration got so far out of hand that Judge Robert Coleman was forced to declare a mistrial in the murder case before him. Whitney climaxed his "show of wealth" by tearing up a $100 bill in the judge's chambers, but he wound up being jailed for disorderly conduct.

Her Excuse

DARLINGTON, England (UPI) — Mrs. Edna Snowden, 52, complained to officials of the ministry of transport automobile test driving center that she failed to pass her test because there was no ladies' room nearby and therefore she was "too nervous" when taking the test.

A Meter Maid in Kentucky Issues Ticket to Policeman

SHEPHERDSVILLE, Ky. (AP) — This community's first police "meter maid" may not have the best possible working relationship with her boss, but she knows a parking violation when she sees one.

On her first day on the job, Mrs. Sue Gabhart gave a traffic ticket to another member of Shepherdsville's finest.

"One of the patrolmen was inside a cafe having a cup of coffee," Mrs. Gabhart said. "The chief was inside with him, and they both sat back and politely watched me write the ticket."

The officer also politely paid the $1 parking fine.

Tired of President,
She Changes Name

MINNEAPOLIS (UPI) — June Louise Nixon said she got tired of having people ask her if she was a relative of President Nixon.

Besides, she said, she didn't care for the President politically.

So she went to Hennepin County District Court Wednesday and asked Judge Dana Nicholson to change her name.

The judge said he was a bit offended because he and Nixon are personal friends. They bunked side by side in the Navy, he said. But he granted her request.

She now is Jean Francis Kirkpatrick. The last name was her great-grandmother's maiden name.

Miss Kirkpatrick said she wanted a name with no political associations.

Her new initials are JFK.

Iowa Girl, 12, Asks Governor for Raise

CRESTON, Iowa (UPI) — When 12-year-old Kathy Kessler asked her parents to raise her allowance from $3 to $3.50 a week, they told her:

"You have to write the Government before we can give you a raise."

Kathy, the daughter of Mr. and Mrs. Robert Kessler of Creston, did just that.

Consequently, a letter addressed "Dear Government" arrived in Gov. Robert D. Ray's office, outlining Kathy's plight. She asked the Governor to "tell them they have to" raise her allowance.

In his reply, Governor Ray said the matter of allowances would be best negotiated with Kathy's mother and father. "But," he replied, "if they said you have to ask the Government, then you can now inform them that you have complied and written the Government."

He added, "Having three daughters of my own, I can understand your feeling that you need more allowance."

Pet Show
(To Eat)

KITAKYUSHU, Japan (AP) — Parents were shocked at a pet show featuring tropical fish to eat as well as to look at, but some youngsters ate the fish happily. An English-language newspaper headlined: "Children Love Pets, with a Little Salt."

3 Men Posing As Police Rob French Merchant

PARIS (UPI) — When three gunmen claiming to be police officers knocked at his door, 71-year-old Javery Mussenalli, a merchant, did his best to cooperate.

When they took jewels from his safe, he became suspicious. When they took the $25 in his pants pocket, he began to fear the worst.

They said they would return to complete their "investigation," but Mr. Mussenalli decided not to wait and went to the police.

Wonder What Bait
He Used?

LAROCHE, France (UPI) — Worker Louis Sarrazin was fishing in the Atlantic Ocean when he felt a pull on his line and reeled in a deer.

Sarrazin and his son pulled the exhausted animal into their boat and with the aid of firemen transported him to a forest to set him free. The animal apparently jumped into the sea to escape hunters, firemen said.

Post Office Employee Finds Sleeping on the Job 'Pays'

NASHVILLE, Tenn. (AP) — On a particularly warm day here, a postal employee decided to rest a bit and sat down on the steps of the post office.

Due to a bit of glare, he closed his eyes and set the cup of coffee he was drinking to his side on the steps as he leaned back.

An elderly woman walked by. Seeing the recumbent figure with a cup at his side, she dropped a quarter in the cup.

Man 'Cashes In' On Luck

SAO PAOLO, Brazil (AP) — Arnaldo Bisoni had a ticket for a domestic airliner that crashed and killed 25 persons. He missed the flight because he lacked proper identification for boarding. Feeling lucky afterwards, he bought a lottery ticket — and won.

Right-of-Way Expert Wrong

SALEM, Ore. (UPI) — A Salem man was given a traffic citation for failure to yield the right of way after he hit another automobile. The man's occupation: right-of-way agent.

'Angry Husband' Plagues Taxicab Drivers in Kansas

WICHITA, Kan. (AP) — The police received several complaints from taxicab drivers about a man who was going around in an automobile pouring oil on them and their cabs.

One driver, who said he was doused twice, reported that the man told him that a cab driver had been following his wife around town and since he wasn't sure which cabbie it was, he was going to get even with all of them.

Warning on California Home Cautions to 'Beware of Cat'

AUBURN, Calif. (AP) — A sign on the door of Mrs. Bobbie Hick's home reads, "Our Dogs Are Friendly — Beware of the Cat."

The cat is a two-year-old, 35-pound bobcat named Growler.

Growler is actually not as fearsome as he looks, and often engages in friendly tussles with her dogs, said Mrs. Hicks.

Seven-Year-Old Driver Punished

CLEARWATER, Fla. (AP) — A 7-year-old boy caused an accident while riding a motorcycle recently and was charged with five counts of traffic offense. Justice of the Peace Joseph Clark said that the boy was the youngest traffic offender ever to appear before him.

Seeing Double

MORAGA, Calif. (UPI) — Joaquin Moraga Intermediate School east of Oakland, Calif., has 13 sets of twins as students. School officials say the twins are scheduled into different classes whenever possible to encourage them to develop as individuals.

Drug-Finding Seems To Run in Police Officer's Family

HUNTINGTON, W. Va. (AP) — Police Lieut. Ottie Adkins, chief of Huntington's narcotics unit, has been bragging "like father, like daughter" since his 14-year-old daughter, Vicky, made the department's latest find.

Miss Adkins was shopping with her mother when she noticed what she thought was marijuana growing in a downtown flower planter.

Taking a leaf home to her father, she had her suspicions justified. It was pot in that pot.

The four marijuana plants were removed from the city-owned planter.

Boy, 10, Unsnarls Traffic

SEATTLE (AP) — When a traffic light went out at a busy intersection, 10-year-old Bill Patterson stepped into the ensuing tangle and unsnarled it until a policeman arrived.

Robbers Wait On Customers

REDDING, Calif. (UPI) — Two unsuspecting women customers walked into a shoe store Tuesday as two armed men were robbing it. One of the men calmly waited on the women, then both escaped with $145 and two pairs of shoes.

Police said the men tied up two employees of the Hoot 'n Boot in a back room.

"One suspect kept a gun on the two employees while the other one was going through the cash register," a police spokesman said. "Then two women came in, and the suspect waited on them. But I don't think he sold them anything."

Parishioners Watch As Thief Steals Window at a Church

PHILADELPHIA (UPI) — Parishioners entering the Tindley United Methodist Church for Sunday services thought they were passing a handyman working on a stained-glass window in the back of the church.

It wasn't until one hour later, when the pastor, the Rev. Maron O. Ballard, asked why part of the window was missing, that they discovered the man was a thief.

"We've never had anything like this happen before," Reverend Ballard said. "People have broken windows and we've had burglars, but no one has ever stolen a window."

Cat Sleeps With Chickens

BURLESON, Tex. (AP) — Kitty, a black cat owned by Mrs. C. L. Booth, climbs on the household's chicken roost every night and snoozes with its feathered friends.

Two Floridians Have Job of Taking Shark For 'Walk'

ST. PETERSBURG, Fla. (AP) — Mike Haslett and Bob Gardner have an unusual job at the Aquatarium on St. Petersburg Beach. They take a 700-pound, 9-foot bull shark for a "walk."

When sharks are captured, they go into shock. "Walking" is done to revive them and to get their gills working properly again.

They walk the shark around the Aquatarium's 60,000-gallon oval shark tank, which contains more than half a dozen other sharks. While the two men are in the water, other staff members crouch near the water and use sticks to keep other sharks away.

An Arab in Tangiers Offers To Buy Wife from a Briton

LEIGH, England (UPI) — Terry Barton and his wife, Liz, said they were walking through the Casbah of Tangiers one night recently when an Arab offered to buy her for $3,750.

"At first I thought the whole thing was a joke," said the 21-year-old Liz. "But then the Arab felt my arm, as though he was trying to estimate how much work I had in me."

"I suppose I should be flattered by having a price of $3,750 put on my head. But to tell the truth I was relieved when my husband didn't take the offer."

A Two-Ton Boulder Is Birthday Present

ORADELL, N.J. (AP) — Lori Folley got a two-ton boulder for her birthday.

The rock was once located a bicycle-ride away from her home, and the 15-year-old Lori used to visit it to sit on, and "cry out my problems."

But she was struck by a car while on her way to the rock one day and, though nearly recovered, was unable to visit her "thinking rock" as often as she wanted to.

So when she was asked what she wanted for her birthday, she answered, "I don't want anything else but the rock."

When it was determined that the rock's owner was willing to give it to Lori, the Oradell Department of Public Works and other people of goodwill delivered it to her home.

Loot Is Found in Car; Theft Report Awaited

TOLEDO, Ohio (AP) — Miss Dorothy Carter told the police that someone must have borrowed her automobile overnight.

The police agreed. When she started to work one morning she found two television sets, 23 bottles of whisky, two boxes of cigars, and a locked tool box inside the car.

The police picked up the loot and waited for someone to report a theft.

'Shadowing' Him Is Perilous

ISTANBUL, Turkey (AP) — An 18-year-old boy in Izmit, western Turkey, took offense when two friends trod on his shadow, considered insulting by Turkish villagers. Rahmi Sarpay pulled out a pistol and shot one of them four times and the other five. Both wound up in serious condition in an Izmit hospital.

Detroit Man
Gets Huge
Electric Bill

DETROIT (UPI) — Donald Beverlin didn't look at his Detroit Edison Company bill when it arrived in the mail.

He just went over to the bank as usual ready to shell out the $17 or so he thought he owed.

The 20-year-old suburban Hazel Park police cadet walked up to a teller and handed her the bill, which said he owed $1,718 and change. She handed it back to him and asked:

"Do you want to pay the whole thing?"

Mr. Beverlin said he "just about fell over in my tracks" when he saw the figure and decided he better call the utility.

"I called and told them I play my record player kind of loud but this is ridiculous," he said. "There's no way I'll pay it. In the first place, I can't afford to."

An Edison spokesman attributed the oversized bill to "a billing error" and said Mr. Beverlin would get a new bill.

Barber Pays Boy $5 to Cut His Long Hair

COLUMBUS, Ohio (AP) — Frank Brumage, 15 years old, traded his shoulder-length hair for $5 from Harold Schweikert, a barber.

"I did it on impulse," said the 43-year-old Mr. Schweikert. "I didn't know the kid, but I like short hair."

"He walked by the shop and asked, 'How would you like to get a hold of me?'" Mr. Schweikert said. "I offered him $5 to cut his hair and he said, 'Are you kidding?'"

"I pulled five ones out of the cash register and he walked in."

"Yeah, man, I took him up on it," Mr. Brumage said. "I was sort of tired of long hair anyway."

Builder in Washington Finds One Day When All Is 'Lost'

TACOMA, Wash. (AP) — It was one of those days for A. J. Corwon, a Tacoma builder.

When checking a duplex he owns, he found thieves had stolen furniture and appliances valued at $650. He then visited a building he was constructing only to find $400 worth of windowpanes had been shot out by BB guns.

He drove to another of his duplexes and found that about $325 in appliances had been stolen.

To round out the day, he drove to a building under construction just as a man was stealing lumber from the site. He gave chase but was unable to catch the thief.

Man 'Mails' His Lunch in a Mixup Of Packages

NEOSHO RAPIDS, Kan. (AP) — As Dwight Hodson's wife saw her husband rushing out the front door to go to work for the Santa Fe Railroad in nearby Emporia, Kan., she handed him a small package to be mailed and a package containing his lunch.

He mistakenly dropped his lunch in a mailbox en route to work.

When he reached his office, he found he still had the package to be mailed.

Fellow employees called the post office, but it was learned that a letter carrier had opened the mailbox, found the food and, thinking it was dropped in as a joke, had given the sandwiches to a dog.

Name Appropriate To Job

INDIANAPOLIS (AP) — Richard E. Bass is director of the Division of Fish and Wildlife for the Indiana Department of Natural Resources.

Wife Limit Posted

KUALA LUMPUR (AP) — Malaysian policemen have been warned that they can be fired for having too many wives. The inspector general's office said some men with three or four wives had become inefficient because of family squabbles. Eighty percent of Malaysian policemen are Moslems, allowed up to four wives at a time under Islamic law.

Wife Thwarts Man By Using a 'Safety Deposit Mailbox'

PITTSBURGH (UPI) — John K. Donnelly just wanted a few more drinks.

Unfortunately, his wife objected and when he asked her for some money, she dropped her purse into a mailbox.

Mr. Donnelly, unperturbed, went to his automobile and got a tire iron and began prying open the box. The police arrived and arrested him on charges of attempted larceny.

600 Eggs
Enough, Duck
Turns Drake

LONDON (AP) — Mary, the mallard duck, apparently decided that 600 eggs was enough. She turned into a drake.

Mary, 15-year-old pet of Alfred Gooch, of Woodbridge, Suffolk, started her sex change by growing bright black, blue, and white feathers. Then she produced a black curling tail feather and white collar, like her male companion, William, and stopped laying eggs.

College Coed
Given an A for
Persuasion

NICKERSON, Kan. (AP) — Denise Tipton, a Nickerson High School student, successfully persuaded State Attorney General Vern Miller to come to the school and make a speech, and, as a reward, got an A in her government class.

Denise's teacher had earlier jokingly promised the students that anyone who could get Mr. Miller to come to Nickerson would get an A. Several students had written Mr. Miller, but Denise's letter caught his eye.

"She wrote a letter that was so frank and honest and true that I couldn't turn her down," Mr. Miller said. "She said the main reason she wanted me to come was so she would get an A. That was straight from the shoulder."

When Mr. Miller came, Denise introduced him to several hundred students who gathered to hear him.

'Prettier Pig' Is Sought

CARLISLE, England (AP) — University of Newcastle-on-Tyne animal specialists are trying to produce a prettier pig that will sell better on the European market, "where great stress is laid not only on lean meat, but also on the shape of the cut."

Cow 'Arrested' for Vandalizing a Roof

RECLIFE, Brazil (Reuters) — A cow was "arrested" on the roof of a furniture factory 80 miles from here after it destroyed 200 roof tiles and then became mired in the debris.

The factory owner refused to press charges against the cow, which was escorted to jail after it was lowered to the ground by several men with ropes.

The police had no clues as to how the cow had gotten on the roof. One official jokingly recalled the cow that jumped over the moon.

Blushes Out in London Store

LONDON (AP) — Sam Morris, head of a fashion store chain, hopes to boost his lingerie sales. Morris has seen strong men go weak at the knees when they ask girl sales assistants for underwear for their wives. So he's opened a "blush bar" staffed by men in one of his London stores.

"A man can handle one woman at a time, but put him in a shop full of them and he panics," says 48-year-old Morris.

Of Coyotes And Lamb

HELENA, Mont. (AP) — Ranchers have frequent skirmishes with naturalists over the value of coyotes in sheep country, but at least one Helena-area rancher can still see humor in the situation. The rancher erected this sign along U.S. 12: "Eat American lamb. 10 million coyotes can't be wrong."

Hot Pants to Be Removed

NASHVILLE (AP) — On the bulletin board in a Nashville insurance office was pinned this notice: "Anyone showing up wearing hot pants will have to take 'em off the minute they walk through the front door."

Woman Taking Driving Test Dislocates Shoulder Blade

ASHBOURNE, England (Canadian Press) — Kathy Reade, learning to drive, overdid her hand-signaling during her third attempt at a driving test in this Derbyshire town.

When the examiner asked her to indicate to the right, Kathy shot her arm out of the window and signaled so vigorously that her shoulder blade was dislocated.

The test was abandoned.

Fire Goddess Makes Believer of Woman

HILO, Hawaii (AP) — At least one visitor is convinced of the truth of a legend that says the Hawaiian fire goddess Pele will punish anyone who disturbs her home, Kilauea Volcano.

Officials of Hawaii Volcanoes National Park said they had received a small piece of lava rock in the mail from the U.S. Mainland with the following note:

"Enclosed is a piece of lava brought back by my son-in-law and daughter. They returned theirs after they'd had a car wreck. My husband fell and hurt his shoulder — so before I break my neck, I'm sending it back to you."

The signature and postmark were illegible.

Snails Race in British Pub

LEEDS, England (Canadian Press) — Snails went on a pub crawl when Don Harris organized a snail race in his Yorkshire tavern. The course: 12 inches along the pub's bar.

Car Thief Couldn't Resist the 'Power Of Suggestion'

HOUSTON (AP) — Mrs. H. D. Ratcliffe works for a chemical company here that produces a household cleaner called "Swipe."

To help advertise the product the license tag on her motor car bears the word Swipe.

Someone took it literally. While she was making a business call recently, someone swiped the vehicle.

Pet Goldfish Charged a Fare

WREXHAM, Wales (UPI) — Paul Butler, 10, was carrying home a goldfish in a plastic bag of water when the bus conductor asked for one penny extra "for the pet."

"It is ridiculous to have to pay a bus fare for a fish," said his mother, Marjorie. "But it has its funny side."

"Pets must be paid for, but goldfish do not come in this category," said a bus company spokesman. "We will investigate the incident."

Boy Enters an Unusual 'Pet' in Pennsylvania Farm Fair

WEST LAMPETER, Pa. (AP) — Mike Tollaksen, 14 years old, entered an unusual pet in a contest at a local farm fair — a rock.

Mike had placed the rock in a hamster cage with a saucer of water, bubble gum, and cough drops.

The judge liked the idea of a "pet" that caused no trouble, and awarded him first prize — but took it back when other contestants protested.

'Softer' Rock Music Sought

FULLERTON, Calif. (UPI) — Fullerton High School has a new provision in contracts with rock bands that play at school dances. A decibel meter will be used during their performance and if the sound level goes over 92 decibels, they don't get paid.